WORLE HISTORY S

Worle's Windmill
The Old Mill, 1705-1764 and The Observatory 1765 to 2012

Raye Green
June 2012

Worle's Windmill, on the east end of Worlebury Hill, has been variously nicknamed Baker's Folly, The Retreat, and The Observatory. This is the story of the iconic building and its predecessor with as much information as we have been able to muster to date.

Published by Honey Pot Press
2 The Dell, Worle
Weston-super-Mare
BS22 9LZ
www.honey-pot-press.co.uk

© Raye Green
ISBN: 978-0-9569752-6-3
2012

I wonder how many people, living happily in Worle in 2012, are quite unaware of The Observatory. I have mentioned it to acquaintances on several occasions and am horrified to find that they think I am referring to the public house in North Worle that was named after our old windmill. Anyone who grew up in Worle will recall that in our childhood The Observatory was clearly visible from the High Street. Today it is masked by trees, which is sad. A description of Worle written in 1929 says 'Worle is sheltered from the sea by its remarkable hill crowned with a windmill': an interesting quotation, since the mill had lost its sails by that time and was simply a tower with embellishments.

I have been greatly assisted in the research for this project by Brian Austin, who looked into the background of the earliest owners; by Nick Corcos who wrote an article on the subject 30 years ago and by Paul Sage, the present owner, who allowed me access to his legal documents relating to the windmill. Sincere thanks to you all.

I think it is time to bring this Grade 2 listed building to the attention of the population.

4

Contents

Beginnings	Page 7
The Old Mill on Worle Hill	Page 8
Shepherd or Sheppard?	Page 11
The Mays appear on the Scene	Page 12
George Woollen	Page 13
Goodbye to the Old Mill	Page 16
Circa 1764 -1803	Page 19
The Workings of the Windmill	Page 22
19th Century Evidence	Page 24
1849: The Rogers Family	Page 26
Changing with the Times: Bakers' Folly	Page 32
The Paul Sage Documents 1890 -1983	Page 34
English Heritage Listing	Page 47
Picture Gallery	Page 48
Appendices	Pages 54 – 60

Beginnings

In the 18th century almost every community of any size in Britain was possessed of its own mill to provide flour – the staple ingredient of the bread of life. Many such mills were run in conjunction with a bakery or a brewery. Worle, a Somerset village, was no exception. The village did not have sufficient running water to drive a water mill, but there was no shortage of wind. The pre-dominant south-westerlies provided the necessary power, albeit intermittently.

There is evidence for the area being blessed at various times by three mills.

Vale Mill was a windmill down on the levels at Moor Lane. It was a tower mill, worked by wind alone, until about 1910. The last millers at Vale Mill were both named Thomas Quick, father and son who had worked the mill since at least 1870. Martin Watts' booklet, *'Somerset Windmills' [1975]* provides some detail and background information.

A second windmill appeared on very early maps on Worlebury Hill in the area of the Water Tower.

But Worle's crowning glory was placed at the exposed east end of the hill, above Hill End and the quarry. It is this mill that became, in later years, Baker's Folly, The Retreat and finally The Observatory. It was not the first windmill to inhabit the site, as we shall see.

Probably the best thing to do before reading any further is to make a trip up the top of Worlebury Hill. This can be done by approaching from the south side, via Milton Hill and turning right at the top, past Worlebury Golf Course. Alternatively, the brave of heart could start from the village of Kewstoke on the north side of the hill and make the precipitous climb up Monks' Hill, then turn left, again past the Golf Course. A drive or walk along to the east end of the hill will bring you to the Observatory as it is now called - but was once Worle's Windmill.

The picture [figure 1] below will help you to identify this unmistakable building.

Figure 2: An aerial photograph, mid 20th century, before the 'big build' showing the site of the windmill and its surroundings.

The Old Mill on Worle Hill.

It is easy to assume that the Observatory had no antecedents, that it was in fact Worle's one and only mill, but it did have an older relation which inhabited a site very close by. It was made entirely of wood and reputedly tinker built, so its fate may be obvious to the discerning reader.

The first evidence of the Old Mill is to be found in the local Rate Books. Dr. Nick Corcos, a well known local archaeologist and historian, tracked down this evidence for an article he was writing for *Somerset and Dorset Notes and queries, Volume 31,* reproduced later in this little volume.

The Rate Books tell us that in **1705** the property was rated at the princely sum of £8.10s. – a great deal of money at the time. This entry does not make clear the ownership of the windmill, nor the exact position of the building. Dr. Corcos suggests that it is not outrageous to assume that a mill stood close to the existing tower in medieval times.

The present owner of the tower, Paul Sage, was told that the Old Mill stood in the middle of his driveway on what is now one of the central flower beds.

Shepherd or Sheppard?

By **1730**, the matter becomes clearer, and we meet Dennis Sheppard, often spelt Shepherd. The property is described in the rate book as a Mill and a Bakehouse, which makes good business sense. The Shepherd clan appear in the local registers and in Banwell Manorial Deeds, and were tracked down by Brian Austin. See appendices 1 and 2 – you will need them to keep things clear.

The rate books for **1740/1** and **1741/2** show Dennis Sheppard rated for a mill and Bakehouse again, but at a higher rateable assessment.

The first Dennis Shepherd, son of Richard Shepherd the elder [gent] of Kewstoke, died in **1727**. He left at least four daughters. Margery Shepherd married a chap by the name of Willis, but no more is known. Ann and Mary Shepherd do not appear in marriage registers.

Prudence, the second daughter married William Leman in **1724**. A year later their son, Dennis Leman was born. Dennis lived to be 63 years old, and he married twice, firstly to Ann Gresley and following her death to Frances Rogers. Each marriage produced one child: Dennis Shepherd Leman b. **1752** and Francis Rogers Leman b. **1765,** respectively. This is interesting, since the mill was later run by the Rogers family for many years, as we shall see.

The Mays appear on the Scene

The May family will be a familiar name to anyone interested in Worle history. Thomas May Jnr. is shown as the owner of the mill until his death in **1758**. Presumably he took over responsibility some years previously, but we have no exact date. See appendix 3 for the family tree.

Thomas May junior was the eldest of at least five sons born to Thomas May senior and his wife Mary. By the time Thomas senior died in 1755, three of his sons had beaten him to the grave.

> William b.1715 died at 22, poor boy, and there is no further information.
>
> James b.1717 was even younger, 19 years old and his death on the register is described thus: '*Killed by ye fall of a flat in a groof'*. I have not yet managed to work out what this means.
>
> Edward b.1722 did rather better, lasting until he was 28. He led a full life, marrying Mary Hart in 1743. Sadly, she died in the same year. Edward tried again, this time marrying Hannah Smith of Worle in 1745. This union was a greater success – they had a son, Dennis May (1749-1821) who in turn married Ann Ozen. Their son, Edward May became Parish Clerk, Schoolmaster and baker and was a well-known local figure. In 1814 Edward's son, another Thomas May

was born. He, too, is described as a miller. He died in 1897 at the age of 83. Hannah May, widowed in 1750, remarried in 1761. This marriage to George Woollen was witnessed by Nick Ricketts, from a family of Banwell millers.

John, b. 1725 was the youngest son of Thomas senior. John died in 1758, the same year as his eldest brother, Thomas Jr. John's death is described thus: *'Killed by the Mill'*. This may mean that some accident befell him at the mill or that inhaling the pulverised grain affected his lungs – there is no way to tell. John had married Mary Masey of Coomberrow in 1754. Mary died, still a widow, in 1760.

Thomas May junior 1713 -1758, who owned the windmill in the year of his death, married twice. His first wife, Abigail, died in 1750 when her daughter, Flower May, was only 6 years old. Thomas married again this time to Hannah, but there were no more legitimate children. Flower also married twice: James Shipton of Banwell in 1765 and Joel Bishop of Worle in 1767.

There is much opportunity for confusion between the two Hannahs, each of which married one of the May brothers, Thomas and Edward. We have to remember that it is Edward's Hannah [nee Smith] who later married George Woollen.

George Woollen

George Woollen's ownership of the windmill came about in **1761** upon his marriage to Hannah May [nee Smith] widow of Edward May. See appendix 4 for family tree.

George had been married previously [and confusingly] to another lady named Hannah, who died in 1760, so he wasted no time in finding a second Hannah to provide his home comforts – and a windmill. George and his first Hannah had six children in all, Betty, Joseph and Edmund seem to have lived into maturity but the next three little boys, all named William in turn, died in infancy and were buried in Winscombe. The last little William died in 1760 and it seems likely that this final heartbreak and difficult childbirth may have led to Hannah's death.

On 28th May, 1761, when George married Hannah May, his 3 surviving children were 12, 11 and 9 years old. They were joined in 1762 by a half sister named Ann, who also died in infancy. A sorry tale that was all too common in the 18th century.

At around this time there are references to Bowen's Map, dated 1760, which reputedly showed the existence of windmill on or near the present site. [ST 352632]. The reference to this map appears in several articles about the mill, but I have been unable to find a copy.

Bowen's map of 1756, shown below, lacks the level of detail that would show a single building.

Figure 3

Goodbye to the Old Mill

A further disaster was soon to be visited upon the Woollen family at the Windmill. The mill was built entirely of wood and, as so often happened to such buildings, it caught fire sometime between 1761 and 1764.

The evidence for this fire comes from an indenture dated 25th December, 1764. This legal document is to be found at the new Somerset Heritage facility in Taunton in packet DD\HB 25. It gives details of the conveyance of a small piece of land close to the site of the old mill to George Woollen, described now as a shopkeeper. The land in question was being sold by Mary Bishop of Worle [widow of James Bishop, former lord of the manor of Worle], her son James Bishop, her late husband's brother, Joel and one Thomas Mullens of Long Ashton. All these four worthies had been appointed by James Bishop to dispose of his Manor of Worle upon his death.

George Wollen was to take ownership of the piece of land on Worle Hill ......
'....in consideration that the said George Wollen hath undertaken to build and erect a good and substantial windmill for the grinding of corn on the ground hereinafter mentioned and granted and that a good and substantial windmill may be erected and built as a publick good for the benefit of the said parish of Worle and all other parishes adjacent in the vacancy of the **old windmill lately by accident burnt down....***doth grant unto the said George Wollen all*

that little splott piece or parcel of common hill ground allotted out for the building placing and erecting of a windmill for the grinding of corn by estimation twenty yards square....at the east end of the common hill called Worlhill near unto or adjoining on the east side of the land whereon the old windmill stood...'

The document is signed and sealed by Mary Bishop, James Bishop, Joel Bishop, Thomas Mullins and there is a part of a signature: 'Jn Pigo'. The rest is concealed by a folded corner on the copy, but a look at the original confirmed that this is the signature of John Pigott.

Figure 4: The 1764 Indenture

So, the old mill, that had inhabited the site and served the village of Worle since at least 1705, was accidentally burnt down in **1764**– a story we have all heard before, I suspect. The man entrusted with the task of building a new and essential facility to provide the villagers with flour was George Wollen, who had so recently 'married into the mill', so to speak.

c.1764 to c.1803

Dr. Nick Corcos investigated the history of the windmill. In his article, published in the *Somerset and Dorset Notes and Queries Volume 31, pages 447, 448, 449* Nick reveals the following information which I reproduce verbatim here with his permission:

> *"Overseers' account and rate books happily survive through the 18th century for Worle Parish. They cast some light on the ownership of both old and new mills and suggest that work on the new began in the year following the conveyance, that is in **1765**.[3] Rates show that in **1760** the [old]mill was held by Mrs. Hannah May and that she was succeeded in **1761** by George Wollen in whose favour the **1764** conveyance was made. The Worle marriage register provides the answer to this apparent change by showing that George had come into possession in the classic way by marrying the lady [Hannah May] on 28th April 1761. The **1762** rate is mutilated, 2pp having been cut out just where the mill entry should occur, but rates continue to be levied in **1763** and **1764**, when Wollen himself was overseer, which strongly suggests that the old mill's destruction had occurred in **1764**. By the same token, as there is no break in rate entries after 1764, it seems equally likely that the new stone mill was built in **1765**, immediately after the grant of the site. Wollen, who was again*

> overseer in **1768**, remained in possession of the mill up to **1770** and presumably died in that or the following year, as Hannah [Wollen, previously May] re-appears in **1771** rate and so continues to her death in March **1786**. She, in turn, was replaced as owner by Dennis May, her son by her first marriage, and he it was who held at the time of the Worle Enclosure, **1801-1803** and whose objection gave the first clue to the existence of the old mill."

There are some early pictures of the new stone tower. Martin Watts tells us in his 1975 booklet that a:

'valuable photograph made in 1867 shows Worle Mill at work with four broad common sails. The tower is parallel-sided with a short flight of steps leading up to one of the opposite doorways at floor level. The cap is the typical Somerset gable form, with chain winding gear housed in a tail-box....'

The photograph, in 1975, formed part of Weston Borough Archives. Confirmation is still required, but it seems likely that one of the pictures that follow is the one Watts referred to. Neither is currently dated.

Thanks to Nick Corcos's efforts we have now filled in the history of the mill from 1764 to around 1803, but there is still a gap from 1803 to 1838. We must assume that the windmill and time went grinding on together.

Fig 5 top: facing south

Fig 6 bottom: facing north. No dates available for either.

The Workings of the Windmill

There is one clue about the inner workings of the new tower windmill in the form of a sketch produced by Frank Gregory. It is lodged at the Weald and Downland Open Air Museum in Chichester, but details are available from The Mills Archive. I have been in touch with Danae Tankard at the Weald and Downland Museum and with Elizabeth Trout at the Mills Archive. Their emails are lodged in the WHS *Worlebury and Its Windmill* file.

Frank Gregory is notorious for being lazy about labelling and dating his work, sadly, but he was active in mill research all his life, from a teenager until his death in 1998. The extent of the information on this sketch is the word 'WORLE'. The archive number is FWG 03601-100. Good luck, if you follow it up! One way to check out the reliability of the drawing will be to go up and take some internal measurements. If they don't match the figures on the drawing we shall know that it is not the right windmill. The drawing does suggest a Somerset gable design, but what is a tail-box, as Martin Watts describes? We await further details from the Mills Archive. For the quality of the sketch, I must apologise – it was much worse, but has been doctored so that it is just about viable.

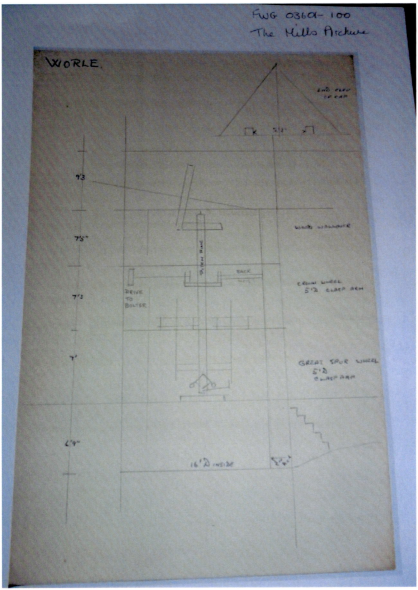

Fig 7: Frank Gregory's sketch of a mill working – entitled 'Worle'

19th Century Evidence

By 1838, where we take up the story, Worle must have changed. There are fragments that can be drawn upon to help build up an image of village life at the time.

Peter Johnson and Derek Venn have done a considerable amount of work on this period, bringing together the Tithe map and the Census information. Their work gives us some interesting figures. 885 souls appear on the 1841 census, of which 466 were male and 419, female. Of this number about half were under 21 years old. These folk lived in 178 houses scattered between Ebdon Bow in the north-east and the embryonic Turnpike Road in the south-west. Sixteen of these houses are described as uninhabited, which may be literally true or may mean the occupants were not at home on census day.

I think it is safe to suggest that it is this population, many of whom worked the land, who would have been the main users of the windmill, together with arable farmers from the outlying districts.

1838 Tithe map identified the land parcels around the windmill as follows:

Tithe Number	
276	Arable
494	House and Garden
496 +502	Orchard
582	Windmill + adjoining land

1841 The census gives Edward May as the known Miller. He was 57 years old and lived with his wife, Sarah, 55 and five children, Dennis 20, James 20, Ann 15, John 15 and William 10. It seems the couple may have had 2 sets of twins. Edward died sometime in 1845.

1845 There is a Conveyance, dated 27 December, from the trustee of the will of Edward May to Matthew Day Jnr.

See Fig 8, below.

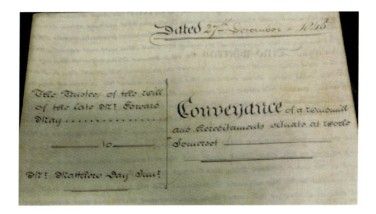

There is no information at the moment about Edward's widow and offspring, or where they lived after the death of the man of the house. However, we do know that the new owner, Matthew Day Junior, immediately signed a mortgage agreement with Sutton and Chalmers for £350.

1845 29th December. Mortgage document from Matthew Day to to Sutton and Chalmers for £350.

Matthew Day lasted for almost 4 years as the proud owner of the windmill. Did he work it as a miller, or did he merely own it and rent it out to someone else?

> *[It is possible that he was renting the mill to Wm Rogers. This speculation is based on Mr. Roger's claim, in 1870 in his advertisement in the Mercury, that he had been working the mill for 30 years.]*

When the time came to part with the mill, Mr. Day's mortgage company signed the conveyance. It was a moment that sealed the fate of Worle's windmill for over two decades.

Fig 9

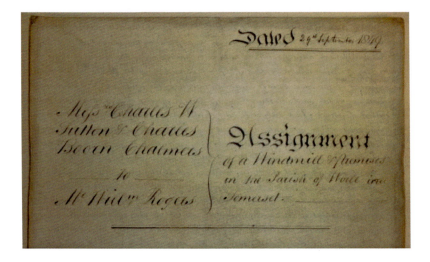

1849: The Rogers Family. On 29th September there is an assignment of windmill and premises from Sutton and Chalmers to William Rogers. See Figure 8 and Appendix 5.

William Rogers was unable to pay for the premises outright, so, on 13th October 1849, he took a mortgage from Edmund May. I have not yet established any relationship between Edward and Edmund. There may be none, but I suppose the May family had always had an interest in the mill. They were brewers, of course, and breweries were often run in conjunction with a windmill, so there is some logic in the association, and the arrangement between the Rogers and Mays only concluded after a further 23 years.

1851 The census in this year gives us some more information. Williams Rogers was listed as 29 years old, and had been born in Worle in 1822. He was married to a young woman named Ann, who was from Congresbury. At this time there were no children of the union, so the couple could concentrate on making a success of the windmill. It would have been usual for William and Ann to be married in Congresbury, near the bride's home, but we have no knowledge about this. If St. Martin's was the chosen venue it is likely that Rev. Nathaniel Wodehouse conducted the ceremony. He was vicar of Worle for 40 years.

1861 The cottage next to the windmill saw the growth of the Rogers family of over the previous 10 years. William [39] and Ann [33] were now approaching middle age by the attitude of the times. They had enthusiastically added to the family, but had not been excessive in Victorian terms. The census lists three sons, Oliver 9, Albert 7 and Tom 4. Their daughter, Alice, was a year old. William was listed as a miller and baker. I wonder how the business was organised. Did Ann look after the bakery? She would have been hard pressed with 4 children to see to. Oliver and Albert were both described as scholars in any case. The school next the church did not begin until 1865, so they must have attended a 'Dame School' somewhere in the village.

1870 Advertisement in Mercury, dated 5th March.

> *To be let or sold with immediate possession that well established and valuable windmill on Worle Hill and in an extensive trade. Also garden adjoining.*
>
> *The mill contains one pair of stones, two dressing smut machines, is in complete repair, has a baker business in connection with it, and is only given up by the proprietor on account of ill health, the mill having **been in his possession for 30 years**. It is one mile from Worle Railway Station and two from Weston-super-Mare.*
>
> *Applications to Mr. William Rogers, Miller and Baker, Worle.*

This must have been very tough for the family. The windmill and its 'premises and land' had been their home for the entire lives of the children. To add to their troubles, there seems to have been some difficulty in selling it. The mill is described as being in good repair and well appointed, but the bottom had fallen out of the trade, and no buyers or tenants came forward to take it over.

Martin Watts speculates that the Repeal of the Corn Laws in 1846 was responsible for the demise of many a windmill in England. It resulted in much cheaper grain from the Americas flooding the market in huge quantities. Steam powered mills were set up and this particularly affected the coasts of the Bristol Channel, since much of the imported grain arrived in Bristol. Added to this problem, many farmers were changing from arable to pasture so the demand for milling dropped like a stone. Sorry! The 1850s and 1860s had been decades when a series of increasingly bad harvests led to a further drop in acreage given over to crops. In fact, when you look at the overall situation, poor old William Rogers' enterprise was never going to thrive long term and be a legacy for his family. It must have been a constant fight to keep going, and this, together with the lung problems that millers often developed from inhaling the clouds of flour, must have affected his health.

1871 By the time the census forms had to be filled in, the business still had not sold. William, by this time, was 49 and Ann was 43, still young by today's standards, but getting on a bit in Victorian England. The family was described as living in a 'house and shop' in Church Road, not at the windmill's cottage. Oliver had left home, but Albert and Tom were both registered as millers, so I dare say William was able to ease up somewhat. Alice was an eleven-year-old, but is not listed as a scholar, so I expect she helped her mother.

In the end, Mrs. Susannah May, Edmund's widow, took over the ownership of the windmill for the sum of £400. The old association was still in evidence. Did Mrs. May take over the place out of the goodness of her heart, or did she have plans for it?

1872 16th February. Assignment of windmill and premises from Wm Rogers to Mrs. S. May.

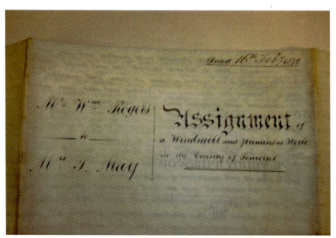

Fig 10, above: cover page of assignment

1881 Census gave Ann, now a widow, as living at Hill End and working as a grocer's assistant. She was 53 and still had her youngest boy, Tom, living with her and earning his living as a clockmaker. He was 24 years old.

At this point we lose sight of Ann. There is an Ann Rogers mentioned in the censuses of 1891 and 1901, but the ages and other details do not coincide, and further investigation is needed.

*****

Changing with the Times: Bakers' Folly

Once William Rogers and his clan gave up milling there is no further reference to be found of Worle Mill grinding grain. Times had changed and the windmill changed with them.

Some time, probably in the **1880s, Samuel Baker** bought the windmill and set about it in a whirl which would do the twenty-noughties justice. He renovated the old building, and built the 'crestellations' which raised the height. He could not add as much height as he had planned because the foundations would not support the extra weight. George Wollen had obviously been rather mean there – not as substantial as we thought, then. The sails were removed around this time, though we have no exact date, and a copula was added to the top. The place was advertised variously as an observatory and a tearoom. The advertisement that follows is a wonderful demonstration of the early machinations of the imaginative mind.

> *From the Tower and Grounds charming views may be had of the surrounding scenery for upwards of a 50 miles radius.*
> *Accommodation for very large parties*
> *Refreshments at reasonable charges*
> *A walk through the Weston Woods or a drive on the Upper Bristol Road brings you to it.*

The drawing, fig. 11, accompanied the advertisement for Mr. Samuel Baker's new venture.

Fig 11

I can imagine Ann Roger's reaction. I expect she shared her feelings with the whole village.

The venture was not a roaring success, and the Tower, as it became known on maps, earned its first nickname – **Baker's Folly.**

*****

The Paul Sage Documents

I was recently [2012] fortunate enough to visit Paul Sage, the present owner of the Observatory and its related premises. He allowed me to borrow 2 packets of 66 legal documents relating to the Observatory that spanned its history from 1890 to 1983. The essence of this evidence is dealt with in this section.

1890 19th August. Conveyance from Samuel Baker to William Jones.

Perhaps the constant references locally to 'Baker's Folly' was the final straw that led to the sale. It seems to be locally acknowledged that the tearoom had not been a success.

1901 16th October. Conveyance from Wm Jones in the first part to George Gunning, Mary Ann Gunning and Wm Jones in the second part.

Presumably, the Gunnings were persuaded to go into business with W. Jones. Interesting to see such a well known local name was associated with the building. The only story I have about this time is that the Observer Corps made use of the building during World War 1. This is said to have led to it being known as the Observatory. Whilst it may be true that it was used in this way, it had been referred to as the Observatory some 20 years previously in the 1890 document. It does, however, suggest that it was no longer used as a commercial venture at this time – another avenue which needs more research.

With the Great War finally over, the Observatory again changed hands.

1919 21st July. A Reconveyance took place from Wm Jones [still going strong] to W. G. Gunning and Fredk Gunning of Dusty Forge Inn, Ely, nr. Cardiff.

These Welsh Gunnings became the new owners, but not for long. They must have had plans for it because less than a month later they sold it.

1919 14th August. W. G. and Fs Gunning sold it to Mary Jane Sherman [wife of Charles Henry Sherman, mortgagor], who borrowed a mortgage of £300 from Catherine Edwards, of 19 Llanwit Road, Treforest, Pontypridd, Glamorgan, for the purchase.

It is interesting to note that the premises seem to have had an appeal for women, who were able to arrange the finance to complete the purchase. The First World War may well have influenced the ability of women to take a more public profile and dabble in property and business but they still needed the support of their husbands to complete this investment.

There is a very attractive drawing of the building in its immediate setting, executed in 1919 by S. Loxton. Maybe it was done to help in one of the sales above. If so, either Wm Jones or the Gunnings family may have paid for it to be done. Another possibility is that Jane Sherman wanted the picture to show off her new possession.

Fig 12: S. Loxton sketch, 1919

1925 17th February. Reconveyance between M J. Sherman and C. Edwards, but it didn't last.

1926 7th January. Mary Jane Sherman sold the buildings and land, now referred to as **'The Retreat'**, Worle to Emily Jane Harris of Royal Arcades in Weston.

Within two years Mrs Emily Harris decided to borrow against her property. Sir George Duncan Gray was the chosen lender of £500, as shown below:

1927 28th November. Legal Charge on property between E. J. Harris [borrower] and Sir George Duncan Grey of Weston-super-Mare [lender].

Sir George Duncan Grey was a solicitor, practicing at Grey and Co., 1 Boulevard, W-s-M. Two weeks later, Sir George off-loaded some of his risk as shown below.

1927 15th December. Sub mortgage between Sir George Duncan Grey [borrower] and the said Sir Duncan G. Grey and Herbert Willie Southcott [lenders] £470.

Fig 13, below is a hand drawn plan of the land and premises at this time. The original is on ordinary brown paper, and very delicate. Ref Ob.Doc3 in the Worle History Society Archive.

1927 November 28th: Legal Charge between Mrs. E. J. Harris and Sir G. Duncan Grey and, in the same document the sub-mortgage b etween Sir G. Duncan Grey and Sir G. Duncan Grey and Another. **One photo, ref. Ob. Doc4 WHS archive.**

1928 December 31st: Conveyance from Mrs E. J. Harris to Mrs. Kate Beck. **2 photos, OB Doc5.**

1928 December 12th: Official searches for above. Emily Jane Harris, George Duncan Grey, Herbert Willie Southcott.

1936 May 8th: Supplemental Abstract of the Title of Mrs Kat Beck to freehold site known as 'The Retreat' otherwise 'The Observatory' Worle. Handwritten. **3 photos, Ob Doc8..**

1936, May 21st. 'All that piece or parcel of land being part or parts of the Worle Hill in the Parish of Worle nos. 258 and 259 on the Ordnance Survey Map 1903 and 1930 editions for the said Parish and containing 3a. And 26p. more or less Together with the messuage and outbuildings erected thereon or on some part thereof and known as 'The Observatory' Worle. Note attached says 'Drainage of the premises is to a cesspool.'

1936 May 21st: Official search application. Kate Beck shown as a widow who owned The Abbey, Banwell, The Observatory, Worle and The Paddocks, Iver, Bucks.

1936 May 25th: Conveyance from Mrs. Kate Beck to Cyril J. Pickering.

1936 June 30th: Official Search shows Cyril John Pickering as a Company Director

1938 August 16th: Reconveyance between Midland Bank Ltd and Cyril John Pickering. **Photograph of the schedule. Ob Doc 12.**

1938 August 17th: Official search for Cyril John Pickering, Company Director

1939 April 29th: Official search for C. J. Pickering, now a 'gentleman'

1938 August 17th: Mortgage between C. J. Pickering and Lloyds Bank Ltd. Also dated May 1939.

1939 April 29th: Official search in respect of no. 16 below.

Mrs Elizabeth Lewis owned the Observatory throughout the early years of World War 2. She may have been in residence during the years when Worle Home Guard used the tower as a picket post, but it is generally thought that the Pickerings continued to rent it. The men of the Home Guard were stationed at the premises, especially on night duty, in groups of 3. It was also used for all sorts of training purposes and was a valuable look out post, with its extensive views.

The two small pictures [fig 13 & 14] were taken on a visit in 2012, but, allowing for inevitable changes, they demonstrate the usefulness of the position.

1939 May 2nd: Conveyance from C. J. Pickering to Mrs. M. E. Lewis.

Figs 13 and 14, taken 2012

1940, On 18th September, a tragedy occurred at the Observatory Picket Post. Three men of Worle Home Guard were on night duty at the tower- Jack Crocker Raines, Harold Singleton and Frank Meakin were all carrying arms. Blackout was in force and when one of the men needed to open the door to go outside the lights had to be switched off. Harold Singleton shouted that he could not see what he was doing with his gun, and at that moment a shot rang out. Jack was shot in the groin. His femoral artery was severed and he died later that night in Weston hospital with his wife at his bedside.

It was a disaster for the Home Guard and the village. Jack's funeral took place at St. Martin's and was attended by 300 people.

The Observatory continued to be used for Home Guard matters but I imagine that night duty at the Observatory was looked upon with grave misgivings after that.

Elizabeth Lewis remained the owner until the Summer of 1944, when she sold it to William and Daisy Payne.

1944 August 21st: Agreement for sale by Mary Elizabeth Lewis to William David Payne and Daisy Payne.

1944 September 11th: Official search

1944: Supplemental abstract of Title of Mrs. M. E. Lewis to the freehold land and premises known as 'The Observatory' Substantial document with plan attached. 12 pages. The plan in question is shown as Figure 13, on page 28.

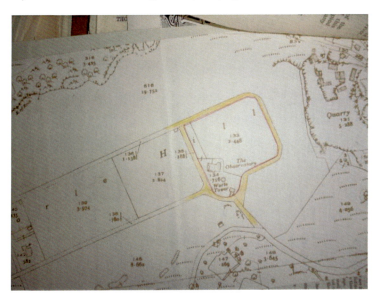

Fig 15

The plan at , fig. 13 is dated around 1944 and gives us some idea of the area around this time. It is interesting to notice that the old windmill is labelled 'Worle Tower', whilst the entire property seems to be known as 'The Observatory'. It is also possible to get some idea of the extent of the quarry.

1944 September 13th: Official search, Mary Elizabeth Lewis of 'The Observatory' Worle and of 'Broadway', Nottage, Porthcawl, Glam. William David Payne, Gentleman and his wife, Daisy both of Elm Tree Hotel, WsM

1944 September 21st: Conveyance between 'Mrs. M.E. Lewis and others' and Hugh Curling Doddrell Esq. Of Tranquil Corner, Betchworth, Surrey. £4,100

1946 May 7th: Official search

1946: Abstract of Title from 1901 to 1944 together with plan of site.

1946: Copy of abstract at no. 24 above

1946 July 31st: Official search of Hugh Curling Doddrell, 'The Observatory', formerly of Beckington Castle, Beckington, Somerset, and of Betchworth, Surrey

1946 August 8th: Conveyance from H. C. Doddrell Esq., to C. J. Pickering, Esq. Of 37 Oxford St. WsM. £5,650

1946 May 27th: Reconveyance between Midland Bank Ltd and Cyril John Pickering. **Photograph of schedule, Ob Doc 28 Packet B**

1949 May 28th: mortgage Mr. C. J. Pickering to Ramsbury Building Society. £4,500. There is a note on the front next to Mr. Pickering's name which says 'now Jarrett'. Photo of back of document '.......all monies intended to be secured by the within written deed, payment have been made by George

William Jarrett the person entitled to the immediate equity of redemption. This receipt shall not operate as a transfer...

1949 May 24th: Official search Cyril John Pickering

1950 November 1st: Second Legal Charge between C J. Pickering [the borrower] and Emile Claud Pollock Lalonde [the lender] £600

1950 May 7th: Official Certificate, C J. Pickering. Photo

1952 May 12th: conveyance from C. J. Pickering, Esq. To G. W. Jarrett Esq. Of 27 Cecil Road, and the Ramsbury Building Society.

1952 March 31st: Official search of The Observatory, Worle in the occupation of Cyril John Pickering.

1952 April 3rd: Enquiries of Local Authority. Official search in Local Land Charges Register

1952 April 7th: Letter from Borough Council about the Official Search about the road next to the property, which had not been adopted by the council.

1952 Supplementary Abstract of Title of C. J. Pickering.

The Pickerings remained in residence at the Observatory until the early 1950s. Miss Pickering was the local music adjudicator for Worle Secondary School, and is remembered by Peter Snook, an old pupil of the school, as driving an Armstrong Siddeley Hurricane Convertible. Wow. I have allowed myself to deviate somewhat from the main topic in order to look at an example of this wonderful car, pictured over the page.

Fig. 16

1960 September 19th: Official certificate of no. 38.

1960 October 20th: Official search

1962 October 12th: Official search

1962 October 15th: Official certificate that the search has been made. Strange attachment, printed white on black referring to Annie Saddler of Springfield House. Photo.

1962 October 16th: Official search of George William Jarrett, 'Cliffs' Cliff Road WsM, gentleman's outfitter

1962 October 19th: conveyance from G. W. Jarrett to Mr. M.C. Thornton and Mrs. A Thornton, both of 59 Worlebury Hill Road. £12,000

1965 June 3rd: Official search of land registry numbers 133 and 134 on Ordnance Survey Map [1936 revision] Map attached. Photo.

1965 June 3rd: Official search

1965 July 13th: Peal Assurance Policy

1965 September 16th: Letter from John Hodge and Co re. Purchase of The Observatory for £14,800

1965 September 17th: Official search Michael Crowther Thornton of 59 Worlebury Hill Rd and Audrey Thornton, and Sage and Down Ltd. Station Road, Worle

1965. Abstract of Title – 4 pages

1965 September 28th: Letter to John Hodge and Co. re Sage and Down. No liquidation proceedings pending.

1965 September 28th: Deed of Appointment between Audrey Thornton and Roderic Ernest Painter.
Michael Crowther Thornton died on 19th October, 1964, in sad circumstances.

1965 September 29th: Mortgage between Sage and Down [mortgagor] and Mrs A Thornton and R. E. Painter [mortgagees]

1965 September 29th: Conveyance from Mrs. A. Thornton and another to Sage and Down Ltd.

1965 September 29th: Mortgage document stamped 4th Oct 1965. Note on front 'dated 16th June 1966....discharging receipt enclosed'

1966 July 14th: Official search certificate

1966 November 14th: Official search

1966, November 14th: Official certificate of search

1967 February 9th: Letter from Ordnance Survey about re-triangulation. Permission for Brass Bolt was granted by Mrs. Lewis on 4/4/44 and was still essential. **Photo Ob Doc 58**

1968 July 31st: General Accident insurance documents.

1972: Draft Agreement between Sage and Down Ltd and Paul George Edward Sage for option to purchase.

1972 Oct 3rd: Agreement relating to Option to purchase The Observatory.

1973 January 2nd: Reconveyance between Midland Bank and Sage and Down. **Photo of schedule, Ob Doc 62**

1983 May 11th: Planning application for a garage passed

1983 May 19th: Department of Environment letter about listing the building. **Copy made**

1983 July 5th: Letter about land adjoining the Observatory

1983 September 5th: Letter and documents from Woodspring D. C. about the listing.

End of Paul Sage Documents.

*****

English Heritage Listing of the Observatory
1983 May 19th : IOE Number: 33264

Worle Tower Observatory, Worlebury Hill Road, was added to the National Heritage List for England as a Grade 11 listed building. The listing details for the building are as follows:

Worlebury Hill Rd 1.5121 Worle Tower Observatory
St. 36 SW 1/76 II 2.
Probably late 18th century. Formerly a windmill. Converted circa 1876 to an observatory.
Circular, 3 stage tower. Rendered. Corbelled battlement parapet. Upper windows have slight ogee moulding cut into the lintel. Door set back in slightly splayed opening with moulded lintel.

It is almost 30 years since the building was listed and in that time it has been cared for by Paul Sage. It is now a very smart and highly unusual garden shed, which has to be looked after according to the rules laid down by English Heritage.

The tower, which could once be seen from the High Street, is now obscured by trees, but the walk up the hill, or along Worlebury Hill Road, is worth every moment. There are some seats at interesting vantage points where one can sit and admire the views over the Bristol Channel to Wales, or across the levels to the Mendips.

The 2 photos that follow are not dated, but may wet your appetite.

Fig. 17: No date for this picture

Fig 18: Apparently decorated for a Royal occasion, but which one?

Fig. 19: 2012. This interesting old log is standing on the tiled ground floor of the building. It is thought that it was originally a lintel above one of the first floor windows.

Fig 20: 2012. The top of the stairs from the ground floor to the first floor with the window where the lintel was in days gone by.

Fig 21: The ceiling of the top floor, replaced by Paul's father 30 odd years ago.

Fig 22: Paul Sage, the current owner, standing on the roof with battlements

Fig 23: Pristine in 2012, thanks to Paul's tender, loving care.

Appendix 1.

Dennis Shepherd in Banwell Manor Record Book of leases, usually 'for the lifetime of....'

1716 Dennis for lives of Jane, wife of Josias Star and Jn° Cook, son of Jn Dec^d

****

1692 8 acre Mead and Pasture. Dennis son and heir of Richard dec^d for self and for Ezekiel Shepherd s. of Edmond of Worle.

1710 Dennis for self and daughters Margery and Prudence

1731 5 acres – part of 8 acres to Wm Leman for wife Prudence, son Dennis and Margery Willis

****

1709 Munday Land and Colethorpes Cottage to Dennis for live of Mary, w. of Wm Shepherd; her son Thos Symons, and for Jn Caple of Worle

1712 re Colethorpes [first 1666] to Josias Star and wife Jane For Ann, Mary and Prudence, dters of Dennis.

****

1664 Dennis son and heir Richard dec^d for lives of Edmund Busher and Edm^d of Worle and Walt Millard and Jn of Worle

1710 Dennis – for lives of himself, his dtr Margery and for Walt Millard of Worle

1721 Dennis – for self, his dtrs Margery [Mrs Willis] and Prudence.

****

1695   *re The 7 acres.   Dennis [for his life only]*
For self, wife Susanna, and John Fry the Younger of Worle
****

1688   *Dennis as s. and h. Richard dec^d grants 'Overland 3 acres' Worle to lives of*
Thos Geo Sparey sons Thos of Worle and Nicholas Stone s. Bic. Of Banwell

1721   *Dennis – for George Sparey, Prudence Shepherd, Ann Smith*
****

Early undated: Dennis together with Robert Goss [who d. 1680]

For a half yard	'West brook'	'Towerdark'
	'Ruddocks'	'Wickhams Furlong'
	'Bourgreeton'	'West Allorside'

1703   *Garston $7^1/_2$ acre – Edmund Shepherd for lives of his children Ann and Edmund and for Dennis Shepherd*

Research carried out and supplied by Brian Austin 2012

Appendix 2
Dennis Shepherd/Sheppard family connections

Shepherd as per Registers AND Banwell Manorial Deeds

Edmund Shepherd of Banwell. Gent
|
Richard baptised 1630. Probably the man below by elimination.

Richard Shepherd of Kewstoke 'gent' the elder. Died 1655
m.
|
Dennis Shepherd ???? -1727
Married Susannah ???? – 1729
|
Children include [some died, infants not listed]

Margery	Prudence	Ann	Mary
b. 1695	m. 1724		
m. Willis	Wm Leman		

                        Dennis Leman 1725 -1788
                        m. 1749 Blagdon to
                        Ann Gresley dtr Rev.
                                    M [2] 1762 Long Ashton to
                                    Frances Rogers, 1740 -1768

Dennis Shepherd Leman	Frances Rogers Leman
1752-1807	1765 -1832
Surgeon of East Brent.	

Brian Austin, 2012

> Deeds show Leman family as 'cousins' to "Joseph Rogers family"

Appendix 3

Tree showing the association between the May and Wollen families, supplied by Brian Austin. Original available from www.worlehistorysociety.net

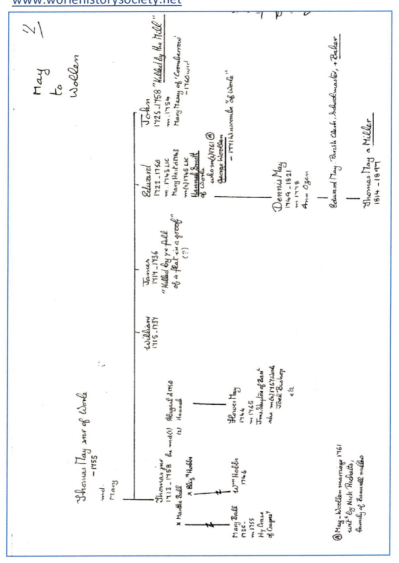

Appendix 4: George Woollen of Worle,
Supplied by Brian Austin

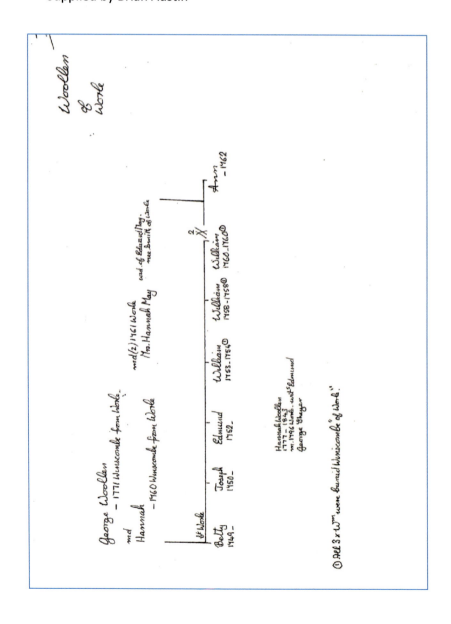

Appendix 5: Tree of the two Rogers families of Worle
Supplied by Brian Austin

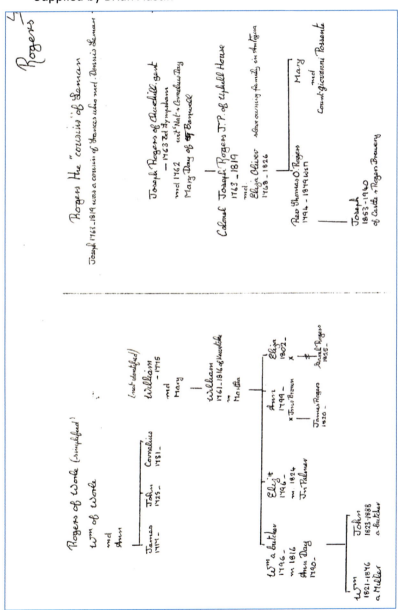